ON SECOND THOUGHTS...

Bad First Ideas and other Rubbish from the Bins of the Famous

SIMON BRETT

ON SECOND THOUGHTS

Summersdale Publishers Ltd
46 West Street
Chichester
West Sussex
PO19 1RP
UK

www.summersdale.com

Printed and bound in Great Britain

ISBN: 1-84024-547-6

ISBN: 978-1-84024-547-9

ON SECOND THOUGHTS...

Bad First Ideas and Other Rubbish from the Bins of the Famous

SIMON BRETT

To Chris Hutton,
an *eminence grise*

CONTENTS

INTRODUCTION

We live in a disposable culture. Never before have more things been thrown away. But, as sociologists and psychologists know, what we throw away is frequently very revealing about ourselves. Tabloid editors employ specialist garbage-sifters literally to get the dirt on the famous. And that's what this book contains – items which, for one reason or another, the famous might have thrown away.

Now the one thing we all know about rubbish these days is that it has to be recycled, so, doing the proper thing by the environment, I have incorporated into this book the pick of material from an earlier volume which was published under the title *The Wastepaper Basket Archive*. But that has been brought up to date with lots more good stuff – letters, sketches, early drafts and deleted e-mails. Here you will find the litter of the literati, along with rejects from the worlds of royalty, politics, science, visual art, music, theatre, television and many others.

Exhaustive research and state-of-the-art retrieval methods have made it possible to present to the public this unique collection of private papers. Some of it is just the detritus of the famous. And a lot is stuff that 'seemed a good idea at the time'. Until someone thought: 'Oooh... On second thoughts... maybe not.'

Simon Brett

Frendes of
Canterbur'ye Cathedrale
Ye Archebishoppe

doth invite ye

to
ye cathedrale onne
ye twenty nineth of
december 1170

for ye

Special
Christmasse Quizze

come and have a Stabbe at
it!

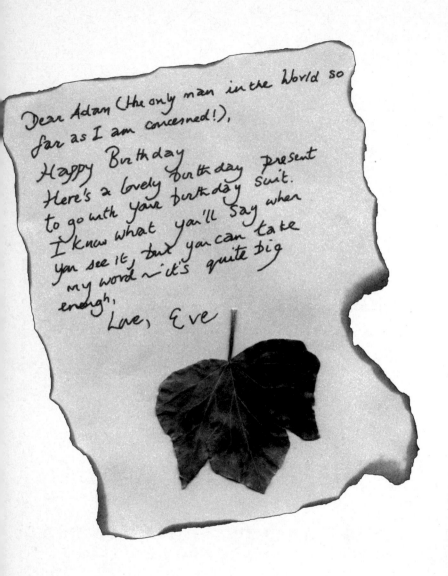

Dear Adam (the only man in the world so far as I am concerned!),

Happy Birthday

Here's a lovely birthday present to go with your birthday suit. I know what you'll say when you see it, but you can take my word — it's quite big enough.

Love, Eve

VR

*17th February
1840*

Albert~

We were amused
by what you did last
night.
Present yourself at the
Royal Bedchamber
this evening at 9:45
precisely and we (you)
will try it another way.

Victoria Regina

(And no more of
your naughty
spoonerisms Albert
Those aren't amusing
they're just vulgar!)

JEFFREY ARCHER

THE WRITEWAY SCHOOL OF NOVEL-WRITING
(CORRESPONDENCE COURSES TO HELP YOU IMPROVE YOUR STYLE

AND LEARN HOW TO WRITE STUFF THAT´LL REALLY SELL!)

LESSON ONE :

The most important thing for any writer to learn is how to tell a JOLLY GOOD STORY.

But the best writers also manage to TELL A JOLLY GOOD STORY IN AN INTERESTING WAY.

And what are the magic ingredients that helps you TELL A JOLLY GOOD STORY IN AN INTERESTING WAY? Well, first of all, there´s a little secret called STYLE. And then there´s another thing called HAVING BELIEVABLE, THREE-DIMENSIONAL CHARACTERS.

So the first aim of this course is to teach you how to develop your own STYLE - to avoid flatness, dullness... well, we don´t need to detail all the things that are often wrong with people´s STYLE. The fact that you´ve enrolled in this correspondence course means that you´re well aware of your own shortcomings in that direction!

Right, so what are your first steps going to be in stopping your writing being turgid and boring? Before anything else, just try READING SOMETHING YOU´VE WRITTEN. Yes, it may be a bit of a shock - not to
rude awakening. Why is it that y
alive, can´t make them jum
inter

18

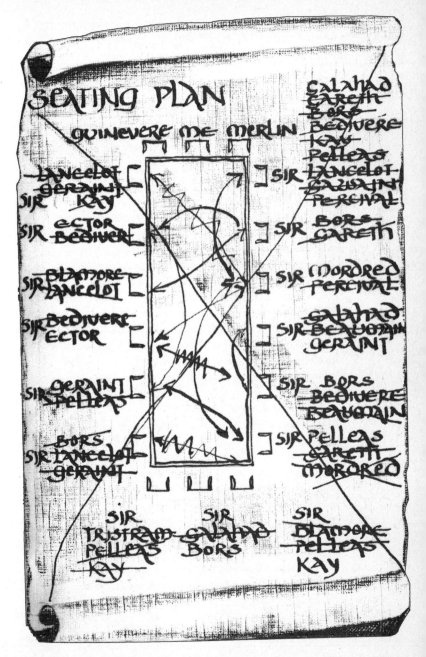

SENSE AND SENSUALITY

CHAPTER ONE

It is a truth universally acknowledged, that a single woman in possession of her virginity, must be in a state of urgency to lose it. Such was the condition of Arabella Moreton, in whom the becoming modesty of infancy:- a reticence of participation in boys' plays - gave way, at fifteen, to much talk of the proximity of the Regiment, and a longing for balls; though these passions were still tempered by a maidenly bashfulness, which disguised an inclination for more heroic enjoyments; an inclination which grew as she entered her twentieth year to a constant excitation; and which, with the approach of her thirtieth birthday, fell but little short of desperation.

The family of Moreton had long been settled in Kent. Though Arabella's parents were not invited to the greatest houses of the county, they were nonetheless on calling terms with many of the lesser gentry; amongst whom the exchange of cards, courtesies, and occasionally wives, was the invariable practice.

Mr. Moreton was a gentleman of considerable aspirations; in mixed company he was all eager delight;- his hands were here, there, everywhere, when young ladies were present; and yet his profligacy remained a matter of discussion rather than execution. As Mrs. Moreton knew, to her cost, despite her own continued exertion of strength and ingenuity, her husband had long since ceased to be an equal participant in those intimacies of marriage, which religion has endowed with its blessing. Like the boastful soldier of classical literature, he devoted a disproportionate number of words to something, which, in his case, was of such minor significance, that it did not in truth merit the dignity of a mention.

1

SENSE AND SENSUALITY

For many wives, this situation might be regarded as a matter for regret, but as one incapable of improvement: an opportunity, perhaps, for a more rigorous concentration on the arts of the needle, the pencil, and the piano; or for the more intense pursuit of those interferences in the lives of the underprivileged, which pass under the title of charity. Mrs. Moreton was not such a woman. When it became clear to her that her expectations within the confines of marriage were reduced to mere civilities, she turned her eye outward, in the hope - nay, indeed, with the firm intention, - of meeting a gentleman of more dependable endowments, whose inclination towards misconduct would match her own.

In this quest, she was quickly satisfied; making the acquaintance of a Mr. Bolney, a gentleman of unimpeachable parts; husband of a lady, who, from lack of interest rather than lack of ability, manifested the same marital shortcoming as Mr. Moreton. Communication was quickly established; and mutual compliment soon transformed this into intimacy; for, when waning charms and flattery are united, it requires uncommon steadiness of reason to resist the attraction of being called the most charming creature in the world. Under such circumstances, a lapse from grace must be reckoned inevitable; particularly when, as in this case, lapsing from grace is, on both sides, already a firm intention.

A regular sequence of *rendezvous* became as nearly settled, as the nature of such arrangements would allow. In the name of card games, and of the healthful necessity of taking as much fresh air as the constitution will accept, Mrs. Moreton and Mr. Bolney contrived to meet with the regularity of church services. Their respective spouses, for reasons of either stupidity or tactics, remained unaware of this exceedingly convenient arrangement; though both benefited from the increased geniality and greater ease, which their partners' behaviour manifested.

2

SENSE AND SENSUALITY

Though, to Mr. Moreton, his wife's new interest remained unknown, it did not escape the observation of Arabella's increasingly spinsterish eye. The discovery brought to her a melange of new feelings; dejection, mortification, anxiety, resentment, and offence, quickly ceding their place to a restlessness of spirit, which she knew could be defined as nothing more nor less than jealousy. If her mother could so easily, and without punishment, succumb to such indulgences, why should they be denied to Arabella herself.

Nor did she lack for other models of behaviour within the confines of her own family. Arabella was the eldest of two sisters; and Cecily, her junior, had shown no diffidence in organising that most important aspect of a young girl's life, which caused her sister such unnecessary perturbation. At seventeen Cecily had eloped to Bath with a handsome young lieutenant from the Regiment quartered nearby, and, when he had abandoned her after two months, she had elected to stay within those fine and striking environs. There, by frequent attendance at the Pump-room, she developed a facility of mixing in the society of gentlemen of all ages; many of whom, charmed by the ease of her address, would, after an appropriate interval, call at her lodgings in Milsom-street; where the smiling and affectionate manner of her greeting, encouraged many to stay, and, with great felicity, to offer money for the privilege. Cecily accepted these kindnesses with gratitude, and was a living demonstration to her elder sister, that, though its propriety might not be commensurate with its pleasantness, such a manner of existence could be a source, not only of enjoyment, but also of considerable profit.

Arabella, then, did not lack models for behaviour; but as yet she lacked that object so essential to all young ladies burdened as she was: a gentleman willing to introduce her to the manners and customs of that country,

3

which she so earnestly desired to visit, but which at times seemed forever to be locked to her.

Arabella was neither weak, nor irresolute, nor lacking in mental endowments. She compared her life with that of her sister; and quickly observed the truth: that, while her own misfortune was a lack of one gentleman, Cecily's only conceivable affliction was an excess of masculine addresses. Arabella resolved, therefore, to arrange a more even distribution of her sister's riches; and, vowing that, in the two months which remained before her thirtieth birthday, she would lose that thing whose continued presence had become such a source of irritation to her, set out for Bath.

Banquo and Fleance

Macbeth and Lady Macbeth

at Hame

12th December 1040 · 7·0 for 7·30

R.S.V.P.
.. The Palace
Forres ..

Come as you are!

Dear Mr Bartholdi
    Many thanks for submitting your design. I am afraid, to be quite honest, here at the agency we had envisaged something a little less flamboyant for the launch of "Frizzy Ice Cream Bumper Cornet". I hope you will be able to place your design somewhere else.
        Yours Irving Schwartz

and sincerely apologise for the
blunder. I deeply regret any
embarrassment my introduction
to you at the Catholic Ladies' Group
may have caused. I had been
incorrectly briefed by the
association's secretary, who assured
me that your surname was spelt
without an E and that both vowels
were Os. I can assure you the
mistake was completely
inadvertent, and hope that you
will be generous enough to
forgive a simple misunderstand
and not hold it against
that I m
of e

JOHN BETJEMAN

SLOUGH

Come, friendly folk, and move to Slough
It's really fit for humans now.
The middle-class and middle-brow
    Will love it there!

Wise men replaced the village greens
With air-conditioned, bright canteens.
Tinned food and lovely slot machines
    Are everywhere.

Build up new buildings in the town—
A house for just deposit down
By architects of great renown
    At easy rates

All hail the fine suburban man.

Who'll live out his allotted span

(With shrewdly sorted pension plan)

    On nice estates.

All hail his desk of polished oak

Where he can sit, a cheery bloke

And always ready with a joke-

    He's such a wow!

All hail the bright young clerks who file,

And do it with an eager smile.

You cannot fault their working style

    In lovely Slough.

They love to hear the music flow

As background from the radio,

And evening times they often go

    To Maidenhead.

And talk of sports and makes of cars

In quite authentic Tudor bars,

And drink their beer in foaming jars—

    Or gin instead.

In labour-saving homes, with care

Their wives dress up and then prepare

The instant suppers they will share

    When hubby's home.

Come friendly folk and move to Slough,

And when you do, you'll wonder how

You lived before. You're settled now,

    No more to roam.

09.15   12 APRIL 2006

GEORGE BUSH (GEORGE@OVALOFFICE.GOV.US)
TO : <TONY@NUMBERTENFOREVER.GOV.UK
SUBJECT : RE: IRAN

TONY, I KNOW WHAT I MEANT.
YOURS,
GEORGE

----- ORIGINAL MESSAGE -----
FROM: TONY BLAIR
TO: GEORGE BUSH
SENT: WEDNESDAY, APRIL 12, 2006 15:09 PM
SUBJECT: IRAN

GEORGE, I THINK THERE MAY HAVE BEEN A TYPO IN YOURS. DIDN'T YOU MEAN
'UNCLEAR'?
YOURS,
TONY

> FROM: GEORGE@OVALOFFICE.GOV.US
>TO : TONY@NUMBERTENFOREVER.GOV.UK
> SUBJECT: IRAN
> DATE: WED, 12 APR 2006 09:03:59 +0000

> TONY, I'VE BEEN THINKING A LOT ABOUT IRAN, AND FOR THE MOMENT THE PROPER
SOLUTION IS NUCLEAR.
> WHAT DO YOU THINK?
> YOURS,
> GEORGE

ENID BLYTON

It was a lovely day as Little Noddy parked his jolly little yellow car outside Big Ears' house. The little bell on his hat jingled cheerily as he walked up the garden path and rat-a-tat-tatted on Big Ears' door. "How nice to see you, Noddy," said Big Ears as he opened the door. "Do come in and sit down."

Noddy went in and sat down on Big Ears' jolly, plump, comfy sofa. Big Ears sat down beside him.

"What shall we do on such a lovely day?" asked Noddy.

"Well, I've got a few ideas," said Big Ears. And do you know - naughty old Big Ears put his hand on Little Noddy's knee.

"You know," said Noddy, "there's one thing I've always wondered about you, Big Ears."

"Oh yes?" said Big Ears.

"It's about your name. I mean, it's a jolly unusual name, isn't it? You haven't even got particularly big ears."

"Well, no, it's a euphemism, isn't it?" said Big Ears.

"A what?" asked Little Noddy.

"Well, a euphemism is like when you say something polite, meaning something that's jolly well not polite," said Big Ears. "I mean, people say my ears are big, but they don't mean my ears at all."

"Oh. What do they mean?" asked Little Noddy.

"I'll show you," said Big Ears and he unbuttoned

33

DUBLIN CENTRAL LIBRARY
OVERDUE BOOKS DEPARTMENT

DEAR : **MR BONO**

The book(s) listed below is/are overdue.
We would be grateful if you could return
the book(s) to the Library as soon as
possible before penalties are incurred. If
you wish to extend your borrowing of the
book(s), please contact the Library either
by telephone or email.

TITLE : **HOW TO BE ME**

AUTHOR : **MOTHER TERESA**

IT'S YOUR LIBRARY SERVICE

BOOKS — FREE FOR EVERYONE

On the 8ᵗʰ of October we drank tea with
Mrs Thrale, Sir Joshua Reynolds and
Dr Goldsmith were also of the company
and we discussed the precedence of
Life over Literature ~
Goldsmith "Which would you prefer sir?"
Johnson "Don't know"
Goldsmith "Nay Sir, but if you were
     forced to an opinion"
Johnson "Never thought about it"
The conversation then took another turn
Reynolds "Sir, do you agree with what
Voltaire has written on the subject?
Johnson "Have'nt read it. Who did
    you say?"
Reynolds "Voltaire"
Johnson "Never heard of him"
Boswell "But, do you not think Sir,
    that literature is the finest
    flowering of human genius?"
Johnson "No"
Boswell "What, then, Sir, may take
    that title?"
Johnson "No idea"
Mrs Thrale then asked for his opinion
on religion, but Johnson said
he had none. On politicks he had
nothing to say, and when

Possible Titles

~~Heathcliff and Cathy~~
~~Cathy and Heathcliff~~
~~The Earnshaw Saga~~
~~It's a Reet Grand Life~~
~~Wuthering Heights~~
~~Moor or Less~~
~~Cathy and Edgar~~
~~The Country Diary of an
          Emotional Lady~~

~~The Earnshaw Concession~~

~~The Secret Diary of
Hareton Heathcliff aged 13¾~~

I like this
one Emily
Branwell.

(Mayhem on the Moors)
~~The Hitchhikers Guide to
                    Yorkshire~~
~~Oh No! Its The Heacliffs!~~
~~How Green was my Moor~~
~~It Ain't Half Windy, Mum~~
~~Carry On Wuthering~~
~~Cathy Come Home~~
~~Together Forever~~
~~Forever Together~~

IDEA FOR A NOVEL?
(Alma?)
Girl living in London
flat has lots of friends
(Christopher?)
Meets man at work
– she falls in love with
him.
He falls in love with her.
Their parents and friends
get on well together.
They get married and
live very happily together –
still with lots of friends?
A bit unplausible.

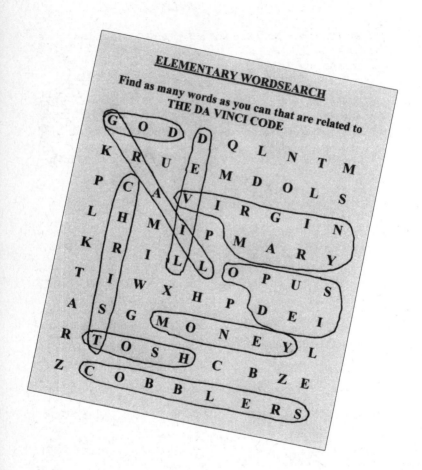

As I walked through the wilderness
of this world, I lighted on a
certain place where was a Den:
and I laid me down in that
place to sleep: and as I slept
I dreamed a dream, I dreamed
and behold I saw a girl clothed
but in a shift, standing with her
legges apart, with a face that
looked like she knew what it was
all about, a couple of buttons
undone at the top, and a great
paire of titties. I looked, and
saw her open her lippes and licke
them, and, as she did, she sighed
and trembled; and not being able
longer to contain myself, I broke
out with a mighty cry saying
Cor! Gette 'em off I could
fancy a bit right, now! And
needed a couple more
and reached her
throbb

HEAVEN

14 JANUARY 2006

DEAR PRESIDENT BUSH,
AS AN AVID READER OF MY WORD,
YOU SHOULD KNOW BY NOW THAT
I DO NOT LIKE TO HAVE MY NAME
TAKEN IN VAIN, AND I DEMAND THAT
YOU STOP PUTTING IT ABOUT THAT
YOU HAVE MY SANCTION FOR ANY
OF YOUR ACTIONS, MILITARY OR
POLITICAL. SHOULD YOU CONTINUE
TO DISSEMINATE SUCH RUMOURS,
YOU WILL FEEL MY WRATH (WHICH
EVERYONE AGREES IS PRETTY
DAMNED MIGHTY). IF I WISH TO MAKE
MY WISHES KNOWN TO YOU ON ANY
SUBJECT, YOU WILL KNOW ABOUT IT,
EITHER BY RUSHING MIGHTY WIND,
BURNING BUSH OR STILL SMALL
VOICE. UNTIL YOU RECEIVE SUCH A
COMMUNICATION FROM ME, WILL YOU
PLEASE DESIST FROM CLAIMING THAT
I HAVE ANY RESPONSIBILITY FOR
YOUR COCK-UPS. AND IF YOU THINK
LISTENING TO THE TUB-THUMPING
OF THE RELIGIOUS RIGHT IS GOING
TO ENSURE YOU GET ONE OF THE
MANY MANSIONS IN YOUR FATHER'S
HOUSE WHEN YOU DIE, YOU'RE IN
FOR A VERY NASTY SURPRISE. NEVER
FORGET, SONNY, WHOSE VENGEANCE
IS.
YOURS VERY MUCH LESS SLOW TO
ANGER THAN USUAL,

GOD

To The Cleaning Lady.

Dear Mrs P. – I am sorry 'bout the mess.
But you know how it is when once I start.
Please tidy up and make it more or less
Presentable, if not exactly smart.
I'm sorry for the stains of bouillabaisse
And where I spilled the plum and
                       raspberry tart,
And also for that mash of peas and carrot
And where I overturned my glass of claret.

Ignore the drunken snorer in the chair –
He is a friend – God damn it!
                    What's his name? –
And just pick up the lady's underwear –
(I can't remember whose, or why she
                              came.
There are so many that I hardly care....
Heigh-ho – such are the penalties of
                                 fame!)
And if my sister's there, please will you
                              rescue us.
It doesn't do to be thought too incestuous!

And, Mrs P, when you have finished that,
Please could you wash the glasses and
                    the plate
And brush the carpet and shake out
                        the mat
(I hope it isn't in too bad a state.')
And, afterwards, oh, please put out
                        the cat
(Or let it in if it has been out late)
And then wake me at noon with
                    that which melts a
'Naching head – I mean a hock
                    and seltzer!

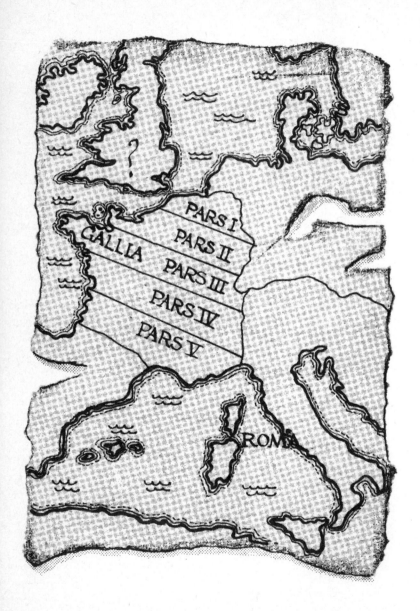

HAMPSTEAD CENTRAL LIBRARY
OVERDUE BOOKS DEPARTMENT

DEAR : **MR CALLOW**

The book(s) listed below is/are overdue.
We would be grateful if you could return
the book(s) to the Library as soon as
possible before penalties are incurred. If
you wish to extend your borrowing of the
book(s), please contact the Library either
by telephone or email.

TITLE : **HOW TO BE ME**

AUTHOR : **SIR IAN MCKELLEN**

IT'S YOUR LIBRARY SERVICE

BOOKS — FREE FOR EVERYONE

WESTMINSTER CENTRAL LIBRARY

OVERDUE BOOKS DEPARTMENT

DEAR : **MR CAMERON**

The book(s) listed below is/are overdue. We would be grateful if you could return the book(s) to the Library as soon as possible before penalties are incurred. If you wish to extend your borrowing of the book(s), please contact the Library either by telephone or email.

TITLE : **HOW TO BE ME**

AUTHOR : **TONY BLAIR**

IT'S YOUR LIBRARY SERVICE

BOOKS — FREE FOR EVERYONE

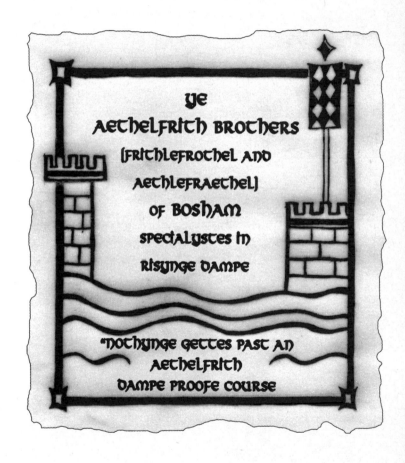

YE
AETHELFRITH BROTHERS
(FRITHLEFROTHEL AND
AETHLEFRAETHEL)
OF BOSHAM
SPECIALYSTES IN
RISYNGE DAMPE

"NOTHYNGE GETTES PAST AN
AETHELFRITH
DAMPE PROOFE COURSE

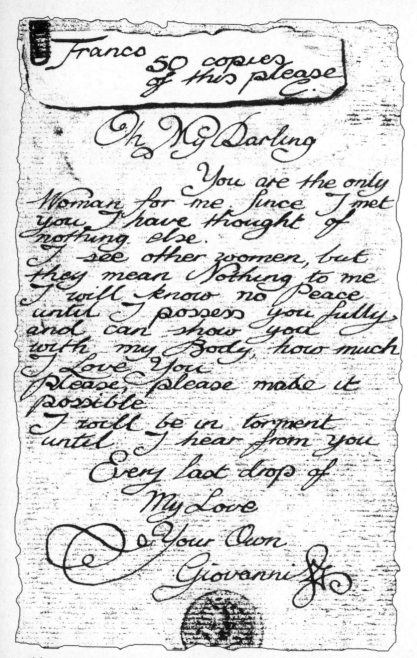

Franco 50 copies of this please C.

Oh My Darling

You are the only Woman for me. Since I met you I have thought of nothing else.

I see other women, but they mean Nothing to me I will know no Peace until I possess you fully and can show you with my Body, how much I Love You

Please, please make it possible

I will be in torment until I hear from you

Every last drop of My Love

Your Own

Giovanni

THINGS TO DO IN MUNICH

1. TALK TO HERR HITLER
2. BUY SOME CHOCOLATE
3. DON'T LOSE THIS
   PIECE OF PAPER.

in a voice you could have scoured a soup pan with.

"Marlowe," I said. "Philip Marlowe."

The girl giggled with private merriment. Her lashes caressed her cheeks. She was neatly put together, and had been told so many times. She wore a navy-blue business suit with creases sharp enough to cut salami real thin. Her dark eyes were cold but looked as if they might come to the boil if the right flame was lit under them.

The man's eyes didn't look as if they'd heat up in a blast-furnace. He was about six feet four with none of it wasted in fat or compassion. The grey flannel suit he wore looked like it was having trouble holding him in. I got the feeling it wasn't only suits that'd have that problem.

"O.K., Mr. Marlowe. So what's your business?"

I said nothing. I let out a little cloud of cigarette smoke and watched it melt in the rather dim light of the office.

"I asked you a question," said the man.

I sank my lower jaw down on to my chest. "I'm thinking about an answer."

The girl liked that. She seemed to like seeing her boss cut down to size. I got the feeling doing a lot of that could be the way to bring her dark eyes to the boil. I also got the feeling it could be the way to get dead.

A flash from the man's eyes stopped her giggle before it dared come out.

"Listen, Marlowe. I don't have a lot of time. Don't fool around. Tell me why you're here."

I put one of my cards with the tommy gun in the corner on his desk. He looked at it as if I'd shoved last week's cheese sandwich up his nose.

"So you're a private detective. What's that to me?"

It was time to hit him with the facts. "I've been hired by Darnley Bombeck to find his daughter."

The facts hurt when they hit him. He gave me a look which ought to have made an exit-wound somewhere round the small of my back. He tried to recover himself, but didn't make up nearly enough ground.

"Why you telling me this. Mr. Marlowe?"

I blew a lungful of cigarette smoke at him. Maybe he'd never liked the taste, or if he had he'd gone off it.

I said: "I thought you might be interested."

He stared at me for a second or two. Then he said sharply: "As a private detective, what do you charge?"

"A hundred down as retainer – that's when I'm working with strangers. Then twenty-five a day, plus expenses."

"That include the car?"

"Eight cents a mile."

He nodded, his heavy jaw brushing against his powder-blue tie. "That's not a lot," he said in a thinking kind of voice.

I shrugged. The girl ran her fingers through her hair. She did it as if she'd rather someone else was doing it for her.

"Look, Marlowe," the man said. "I'd pay a lot more than that for you _not_ to find Bombeck's daughter." I said nothing. "A thousand dollars?"

He let it hang in the air like bait. I shook my head. "Sorry. You got the wrong man."

"Two thousand dollars."

"Ah," I said. "_Now_ you're talking. Give me the

Ye Tabard Inn
Southwerke
2 Aprile 1380

Dear Myster Chaucer
                    Thisse is confirme
oore agremente thatte that thou
shalt have creditte withouten limitte
at ye Inne in exchange for wrytyne
a few lines of poesie to advertise
its vertues—

                    Please say
how goode a hostelrye ye Tabard be,
and how handye in Southwerk for
folk that wolde wenden on Pilgrimage
Saye also thatte we have beddes
for a campaynnge of uppe to nyne and
twenty, that the chambers and the
stables area wyde, and that everich a
man or wooman that comes heere
Shall be esed atte beste. Saye thatte
it sneweth in thus hous of mete and
Drinke (at verye faire pryces)

Enythynge else tho wishest to adde
to ye verses I leve to thy discresioun
but make Soore tho gettest inne ye
aBove pointes.—

                    Yores ryghte Cynceerely
                    F. Smythe
                            Thyne Hoste—

This is
The Last Will and Testament

of me   AGATHA CHRISTIE

I give and bequeath all of my estate and the royalties for fifty years after my death into my dying lost nephew, Eric, from Australia, unless he dies within a month of my death, in which case the property shall go to his illegitimate brother, Henry, the solicitor. If, however, both brothers die within a month of my death, the beneficiary of this will shall be my housekeeper, Winifred Caxton, who is really the daughter of my doctor, Marmaduke Dollington. In the event of Winifred dying within a month of my death, her father will inherit, but only if he is reconciled with his estranged wife, Daphne. If, however, Daphne dies before the month is up, the police should be called and after Marmaduke's arrest, my estate should go to his neice, my long suffering nurse, Betty. Should Betty die in suspicious circumstances

[CANCELLED]

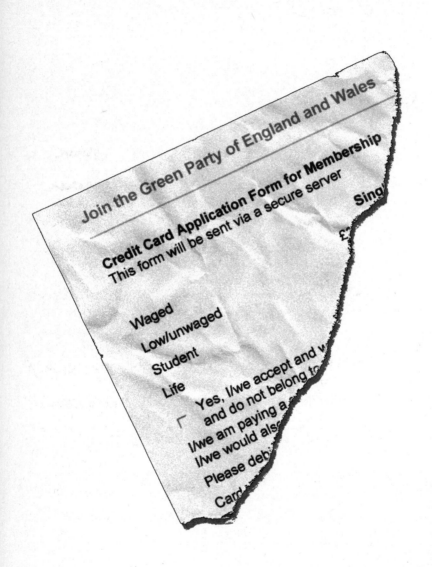

Join the Green Party of England and Wales

Credit Card Application Form for Membership
This form will be sent via a secure server

Sing

£

Waged

Low/unwaged

Student

Life

Yes, I/we accept and v
and do not belong fo

I/we am paying a

I/we would als

Please deb

Card

In Xanadu did Kubla Khan
Prove to be a right Don Juan
        He had Khanal knowledge
        Of nine girls from college —
And buggered ten sheep in a barn

It's no good! Since that person came
On business from Porlock, I just can't
get back into the idiom of it!

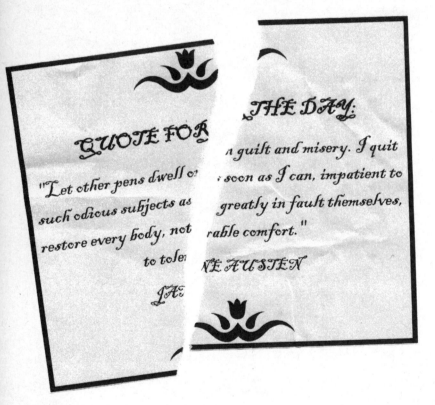

QUOTE FOR THE DAY:

"Let other pens dwell on guilt and misery. I quit such odious subjects as soon as I can, impatient to restore every body, not greatly in fault themselves, to tolerable comfort."

JANE AUSTEN

TYPEWRITER COMPANY

Sales, Service and Repairs

17th August, 1919

Dear Mr. Cummings,

We have examined the typewriter you left with us yesterday, and regret that we are unable to repair the defective "Shift" key.

May we recommend to your attention our latest model, the TITAN, which retails at a mere S147.50, and would be ideal for a working poet like yourself.

Looking forward to hearing from you,

Yours sincerely,

G. L. Biermann

SALES MANAGER

you know nothing's happened
and I know nothing's happened
[and nothing's going to happen
— got that, sonny?] but who's
going to believe that when
you go on writing all this
stuff?

So, for the last time, I
ask you — will you bloody
well stop it! get off my
back! I dare say there are
plenty of girls around who
wouldn't mind inspiring you
but you've got the wrong
one with me — understand?

so stop writing
about me!!

Beatrice

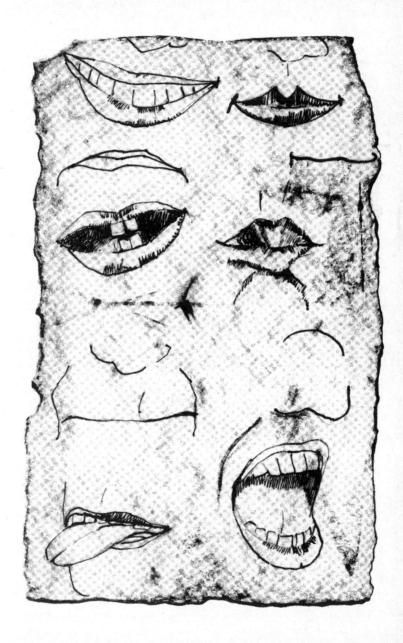

THE LAST CUPPA

Ant is the taller one
Ant is the taller one
Ant is the taller on
Ant is the taller ?
Ant is the talle
Ant is the t
Ant is the
Ant is
An
a

JUDI DENCH

DICK (DICK@GLOBAL FILM AGENCY.COM)   11.15   13 JANUARY 2006
TO : <JUDI@LUVVIEDOM.COM
SUBJECT : FILM SCRIPT

Judi love,
Am biking over a new screenplay just received from Jared in the
Beverley Hills office. You play an embattled but doughty widow and
in this one you don't say 'fuck' till well into the third act. Think it
could be perfect – you know how the British public love you doing
that. Let me know your views.
Yours, as ever,
Dick

THE MYSTERY OF EDWIN DROOD

CHAPTER 23

The Veiled Lady

London. Summer still choking the city breathless. Summer mixing dust with the smoke spilling down from chimney pots. Summer adding the shimmer of heat-haze to this clogging compound of dust and smoke, stirring a witches' brew of bright opacity, veiling, fragmenting and trembling the vistas of towers and terraces, corner shops and cathedrals, bridges and barges, tobacconists and tenements. Summer breaking the images of the city into slivers of coloured glass, changing the picture with the twist of a wrist, like some giant child's hand, experimenting on Christmas morning with its newly-unwrapped kaleidoscope.

Dust everywhere. Dust making tiny archipelagoes on the surface of cold water in bedroom bowls. Dust dulling the shine of tables and cabinets, tall-boys and cake-stands, coffers and closets. Dust in the kitchens, mocking the cooks' mania for cleanliness; dust in the drawing-rooms, caught as slow-moving motes by the diagonals of morning sunlight, biding their time, spinning gently, abstracted, selecting the destinations on which they will descend. Dust in the eyes and ears and throats of the waking world; dust tickling at early morning mouths, calling out the coughs with the peremptory despatch of an usher in a court-room. Dust also summoning up from their cells a dirty company of spits, hawks and hacks.

And dust stirred by the hem of the dress of the veiled lady who walks the early morning streets from the docks towards a hybrid hotel at the dingy end of Cheesemaker Street. Her veil adds another distortion to the refractions of the dust, and London looms, ominous and lowering, like a land seen in a dream, through the unfamiliar net which curtains her face. Her clothes, too, the heavy swatches of cloth across her shoulders, the long swish of skirts against the ground, all feel strange. She seems a creature from the land of dreams, swimming on the surface of the heat-haze.

That behind the veil the lady is thinking, and that the thoughts of one recently arrived from foreign shores must be vivid, is not to be doubted. But can we know the nature of her thoughts? Do they run on John Jasper? Is Mr. Grewgious allowed access to the private rooms of her mind? Does Mr. Crisparkle loll about there, making himself at home, perhaps sitting down in an armchair, with his slippered feet up on one of the mental tables of that secret place?

Alas, we cannot know; and even if we tried to read the mind's construction in the lady's face, we would be frustrated by the dark curtain of her veil.

If her face is denied to us, her hands may perhaps speak volumes of information. Are they the scarred hands of a serving-woman, the white hands of a lady? Do they bear encrustations of jewellery, are they legitimised by a wedding ring?

Alas, we cannot know; for as her face is shrouded by a

veil, so are her hands hidden by gloves of kid.

But let us follow her. Yes, perhaps if we follow her through the dusty doorway of her sad hotel, we may be allowed to share a little of her secret. To the clerk she goes, a moping, fat boy, hardly awake; with almost masculine imperatives, she commands a room. Her travelling baggage will be coming in a fly from the docks; she gives the fat boy instructions for its disposition. Wheezing a little, he leads her up the dusty stairs to a little dusty room. This she surveys, noting with approval the dusty window that looks out on nothing more than an eyeless, dusty wall; and, pressing a half-crown into the damp, dusty hand, tells the fat boy it will serve.

She waits diligently till the descending footsteps have melted to silence, and the fat boy can be presumed to have resubmerged in the torpor from whence she stirred him; then she moves towards the room's one, dusty, mirror. She reaches with one large kid-gloved hand to release the buttons of the other.

Now what will we see? Now will we be granted fragments of the veiled lady's secret? The hands from which the gloves are withdrawn are brown - not the brown of the Brahmin or the African, but the brown of the European unsheltered from a foreign sun. Where have her hands been to return so stained? The curious ring she wears (not on the wedding finger) may tell us. Yes, it is North African work; the beaten silver whorls murmur softly to us the word: "Morocco".

64

Enough of the hands. They have performed their small betrayal and told us all they know. But still they can help us, as they move up to detach the veil and reveal a new informer, the lady's face. It is a sad face they unshroud, a face of suffering; it is a face, too, that, in some way not to be defined, is familiar to us. It is a face that has known pain - not only the distant pains of adversity, but also the more recent pains of...what? Is it illness? Not quite. No, it is a face that has recently suffered the pains of the surgeon's knife.

But can we know why the scalpel, saw and knife were needed? Surely, we insist, it must have been an illness that laid the veiled lady low? Her face denies that; it is too robust, too strong. Her face seems to whisper that, whatever operation she has so recently suffered, it was undertaken voluntarily.

The strangeness of these messages confuses us. Can we ever solve this conundrum, sort out the bizarre contradictions of the information the hands and face have confessed to us? Without more help, I fear not.

But, even as we think this, arrives that help, like a refreshing breeze lifting the dust of this hot, dusty day. The lady speaks, at once untangling the muddled skeins of our conjecture. She looks at her heavy-browed eyes in the dusty mirror, and, with a smile like an evening shadow stealing across her face, murmurs, "Welcome back to England, Edwina Drood."

'I feel happy today,
There's a gleam in my eye,
And in every way
I can reach for the sky.
I feel just as I should,
'Cause my life is so good!'

THE STRAND MAGAZINE

5 February 1886

Dear Dr Doyle.

Many thanks for submitting your short story, which I feel shows great promise. The idea of solving crimes by deduction is an excellent one.

My only quibble though choice of hero. Dr Watson is clearly an intelligent man. He is also a compassionate one (as we see in his treatment of the arrogant dope-fiend Sherlock Holmes), but I'm afraid, in spite of his deductive brilliance, he does come across as rather boring.

So, regretfully, I return your manuscript herewith. Please don't be discouraged. I feel sure that with some very simple changes, the story could work.

Yours Sincerely

J G Penguin.

Editor

BRAINWAVE & BRAINSTORM

THE CREATIVE ADVERTISING AGENCY

23 June 1994

Dear James,

Very good to see you at the briefing meeting on Tuesday. I took on board everything you said about your very exciting new product, and have been throwing a lot of ideas round with my creative boys. We're all in agreement that what you need is a simple but memorable slogan which will really identify your brand in the public mind. After much discussion, we've come up with what we're convinced is a winner. And it goes like this....

DYSON VACUUM CLEANERS REALLY SUCK!

I very much look forward to hearing your re
to what we ar
brand ide

17, Cornhill,
London E.C.

13th November 1917.

Dear Mr. Prufrock,
                    Banking folk
Cannot show very much sympathy,
And your statement is spread out over my desk
Like a body in its shroud upon a table.

You have measured out your life with apologies,
But there comes a time
Between time future and time past,
Which should perhaps be called time present,
When the bank can no longer honour your overdraft.

That is a way of putting it - not wholly satisfactory:
A maybe tactless statement
Of the tired-out financial cliché
"This bank is not a charitable institution",
Not a place
Where hopes can be extended infinitely,
Month by month.

And October was your most extravagant month, spending
Money that was not yours, raising
Borrowings and credit, making
Bad debts with this bank.

I observe, from your letter,
That you have had unexpected failures
Which have turned your sales-graph downwards,
But that you hope to turn again
You hope to turn.

Do not forget,
I am aware that this sort of thing has occured before.
For you each venture
Is a new beginning, a new promise of future prosperity.

I know you, though,
Full of high speeches, but a bit unsure;
At times, indeed, downright dishonest.

Between your promise
And the reality
Between your intention
And the act
Comes the Excuse

I know what you are thinking-
That all we bank clerks come and go
Talking of flow and counterflow.
That
We are the heartless men
We are the stuffed shirts
Grinning together.

But, Mr. Prufrock,
Think of me as you must,
A dry old man,
Wearing a young man's trousers,
(Though I have known the anguish of the miser,
The agony of the spendthrift),
But you do not wish to know
Do not wish to know
My problems.

DO NOT ATTEMPT
DO NOT ATTEMPT TO CASH
DO NOT ATTEMPT TO CASH ANY FURTHER CHEQUES.
Or Sosostris and Eugenides,
Our solicitors,
Will be in touch.

Yours
Sincerely. Sincerely.
        Sincerely   sincerely   sincerely

        T.S. ELIOT

TRACEY EMIN

[Tracey Emin's dustbin is empty, because all of its contents are on display in different galleries around the world. The bin itself is on sale for £200,000.]

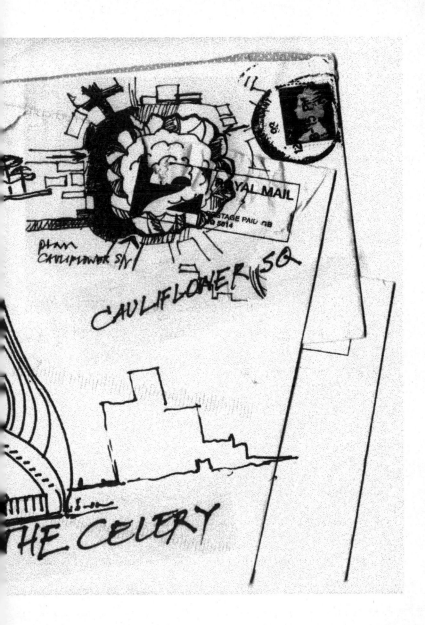

plan
CAULIFLOWER SQ

CAULIFLOWER SQ

THE CELERY

BARON VON FRANKENSTEIN

transyl electricity

GALVANITE HOUSE,
TRANSYLVANIA.
TO PAY, SEE OVER

FINAL NOTICE

BARON VON FRANKENSTEIN,
CASTLE FRANKENSTEIN,
VLADBURG,
TRANSYLVANIA.

QUOTE this REFERENCE NUMBER

3414 093 073 002

Normal reading date

20 OCT 82

V.A.T Registration No. 226 5570 51. No V.A.T. is shown on the amount as all charges for 'domestic' are ZERO RATED

PREVIOUS READING	PRESENT READING	TARIFF	UNITS	PENCE PER UNIT	AMOUNT £ p
3	987b9353213	DOMESTIC	765329721	4.8	45768594322 17
QUARTERLY CHARGE					7 28
		TOTAL NOW DUE			45768594329 45

The amount shown above still appears to be outstanding. Should the account have been paid within the past few days, please disregard this notice and accept our apologies for reminding you of the matter again.

If the amount has not been paid, and payment in full is not received within seven days, the account will be referred to the appropriate department for the issue of legal proceedings and this could involve you in the additional cost of court fees.

C against a meter reading indicates it is your own reading
E indicates an estimate. Any under or over estimates will be corrected at the next meter reading

Payment is now due

SIGMUND FREUD

TO   The ~~Wo~~manager,   17th ~~Orgies~~ _August_ 1904
United Austrian ~~W~~ank,
32, ~~Titts~~_Tehel_strasse,
VIENNA.

Dear Her~~r~~ Kuntz~~l~~er,

     I must apologise for the current state of
my ~~potency~~ _account_. I see from your recent ~~French~~ letter that I
am 23,734 Schillings over~~sexed~~ _drawn_, and I very much regret
~~seeing my parents copulating.~~ _this oversight._

     I can assure you that there is ~~everything~~ _nothing_ to worry
about. I know that the size of my ~~penis~~ _overdraft_ is currently
larger than the facility we agreed, but I hope very soon
to be able to make ~~love to my mother~~ _up the deficit_. Within the next
week I will be paying in the proceeds of the sale of
some g~~u~~ilt-edged security bonds ~~and manacles and whips.~~
I am also owed considerable sums of money by clients for
my ~~sexual~~ _psychiatric_ services.

     Until those payments have ~~come into~~ _come into_ my account, I
will endeavour not to make any further ~~withdrawals~~ _withdrawals_.

     In the hope that you will ~~bare~~ _bear_ with me for a little
longer and extend the ~~full length of your willy~~ _limit of my agreed overdraft facility_ for
another month.

           ~~Whores~~ _Yours_ sincerely,
           S~~UCK~~_IG_MUND FRA~~ID~~_EU_D

NOTTING HILL CENTRAL LIBRARY

OVERDUE BOOKS DEPARTMENT

DEAR : **MR GELDOF**

The book(s) listed below is/are overdue. We would be grateful if you could return the book(s) to the Library as soon as possible before penalties are incurred. If you wish to extend your borrowing of the book(s), please contact the Library either by telephone or email.

TITLE : **HOW TO BE ME (BUT STILL SWEAR A LOT)**

AUTHOR : **MOTHER TERESA**

IT'S YOUR LIBRARY SERVICE

BOOKS — FREE FOR EVERYONE

Dear Dirk

While I am very grateful for the commission you offered me in that rather noisy tavern on friday, I'm afraid I'm going to have to turn it down. I've tried every which way, but I'm having a real problem doing a picture of a laughing Chandelier. I hope that I will be able to work with you again on something less surreal. Groups of revellers, old men, old women and respectable citizens of Haarlem are more my sort of thing, really.

All good Wishes

Frans

Well, Mr Windy wasn't going to stand for that.

"No, Mr. Nosey," he said. "I'm not going to stand for that."

"OH NO?" said Mr Nosey.

"NO!" said Mr Windy.

And then he let fly a REALLY BIG ONE.

Poor Mr. Nosey!

They were sitting in a restaurant in the Bois. They had had a good dinner. They had had good wine. It was a good party.

I walked in. "Hey," Brad said. "You having a good time? We're having a good time."

I rubbed my forehead. "Not such a good time."

"I heard your head was bad," Nick said. "Heard it got bad in the war."

"The hell with the war. My mother says I always had these migraines. As a kid I had these migraines."

"Have another brandy," the count said. No one answered. They all wanted more brandy. "Bud?"

"Hell, no," I said. "I don't drink. Plays hell with my digestion."

"Lots of people lost a lot in the war," Nick said. "Some lost more than digestion."

"Not the war. My mother says my digestion was bad when I was a kid. Nerves."

They were quiet.

"Anyway," I said, "drinking alcohol doesn't do you any good. Makes grown men do damnfool things, like kids."

They stayed quiet. A nigger singer started. People danced.

"Dance, Bud?" Martha said. "I need to dance."

Martha was damn good-looking. She was built with the curves of a hunting rifle, and she knew it. She was a tall girl who sat still with a great deal of movement.

"Dance?" I said. "No, I don't dance."

"Come on, dance. Everyone's dancing."

"I know. I personally don't dance."

"Hell, dance."

"No. My mother knew a young man who gotten fallen arches from dancing."

Martha danced with Brad. He was a good dancer, but not a great dancer. The nigger singer waved at Martha. She spat at him.

Their glasses were empty. They asked the waiter for more _fines_. I asked him for mineral water, regular mineral water, not the gassy mineral water that I drank with Miguel on the Aguilado the time he tried to get me interested in fishing, and couldn't. That mineral water gave me wind. The waiter brought regular mineral water. I drank it. It was good.

"You see the fight?" the count said. "It was a good fight."

"Fight?"

"Lacompte-Frank Martin. He can box, Martin."

"Box?"

"You see the fight?"

"No, I didn't see the fight. I don't see fights. I don't like fights. My mother says boxing appeals to man's lowest instincts."

"Sure," said Nick. "What's wrong with man's lowest instincts?"

I was silent, not silent with the silence of someone who hasn't got anything to say, but silent with the silence of someone making someone else think about what they just said. My mother used to use that kind of silence a lot. Nick thought about what he just said. He was silent.

The music stopped. The nigger singer waved at Martha again. She slapped him. Martha and Brad came over to the table. Martha sat down. So did Brad.

"We had a good time," Brad said.

"We had a good time?" Martha said.

"You're a lovely piece."

Martha slapped Brad. She pulled the felt hat down far over her nose.

The glasses were empty. The waiter brought more _fines_. Martha changed from brandy to pernod. I had more mineral water. It was good, but not as good as the first time.

"Next week they are running the bulls in Pamplona," Nick said.

"Bulls?"

The count smiled. For him the bulls were a special secret, a secret some people would not understand. I knew all about the secret. I was one of the people who did not understand it.

"Will you run with the bulls?" he asked Brad.

Brad smiled. It was his secret, too. "I'll run."

"And if you get gored?" Martha said.

"I get gored. The hell with it, I get gored."

He ordered more drinks. He ordered pernod for Martha. Martha hit him. She had changed from pernod to champagne. He ordered champagne for Martha. I had more mineral water. This time it was hardly good at all.

"You go to Pamplona, Bud? Run with the bulls?"

The music started again. The nigger singer smiled at Martha. She pulled out a gun and shot him. The music went on. People danced.

"Hell, no," I said. "I wouldn't do that for a bet. Bulls?" I wrinkled my nose. "Bull-fighting? Hell, you joking me? It's disgusting. And so cruel to the bulls. Dangerous, too. My mother says that bull-fighting is one of the most degrading and despicable forms of cruelty that human beings

Wolsey, I think this is a righte shitty

Tudorwaye Datynge Servise *idea*

For Companyonshippe Casual Affaires *HRH*
and Marriage

please fille in ye followynge questionnaire

name *henry*   age —   occupation *king*

religion *mine Owne*   heighte *great*   girthe *massyve*

dost thou see thyselfe as

A	comely	aye/~~nay~~
B	sexy	aye/~~nay~~
C	confidente	aye/~~nay~~
D	basheful	~~aye~~/nay

what are thy interestes?

Women, hunting, eatynge, wrytynge musicke.
executynge people who disagree with me
et cetera

what sorte of partner art thou lookynge for?

sexe *female*   age *yours*   occupation *princesse or queen*

religion *mine*   height *small*   girthe *slender*

dost thou wishe thy partner to be

A	comely	aye/~~nay~~
B	sexey	aye/~~nay~~
C	riche	aye/~~nay~~
D	domesticated	~~aye~~/nay

an other special requirements?

Lette her be fertile to beare many sonnes!

what interestes dost thou wish thy partner to have? *none (save mine)*

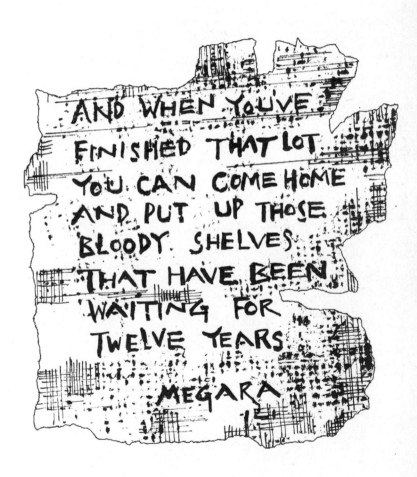

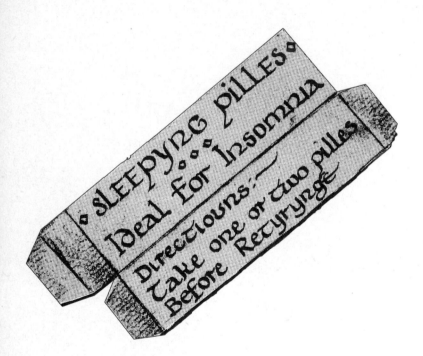

FFBF CLUB
EXCLUSIVE OPENING OFFER!

Someone with your profile gets lots of invitations to join all kinds of organisations, but this offer is different. In the Famous For Being Famous Club's exclusive Central London premises, you will be guaranteed only to meet your kind of people, people with just your amount of skill and achievement. Yes, if you take up this offer, you won't have the hassle of mixing with talented, creative people whose publicity is connected with any actual accomplishments they might have. No, you'll be with your own kind and will not be expected to shine in any

ADOLF HITLER

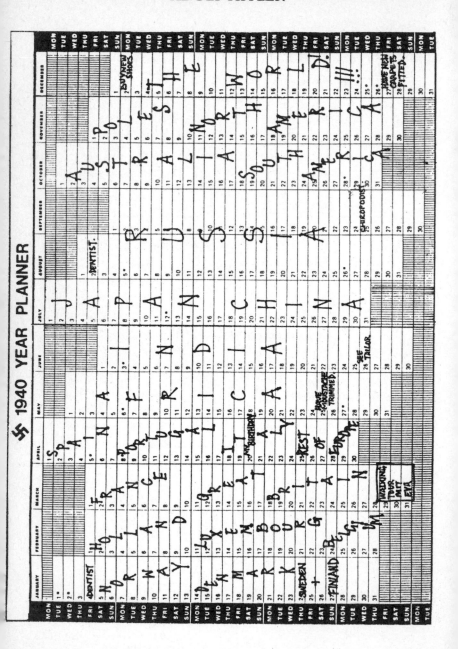

90

SHOPPING LIST

I must this morning's morning shopping buy, stop-
        ping at grossest grocers', gather grained green
                bacon, not forgetting
        Half of red-wrapped Edam, and I'll get
                the Cheddar there (all sweating
High there – how it stinks upon the slab of
                The shoddy shop –
Smell it putrefy!). Then off, off, buy a chop,
        And a cow's heel comes close on my
                long list. Then stakes and netting
        To box the big trees (and thus not letting
Herds of the birds to demolish, to nibble up
                All the crop).
Bread, biscuits and veal-chops and what...?
                        Oh, what? Buy booze, yes...
                        Baked beans! And that fish that flakes
                        From the bone, and cereal...
Quick-cook porridge and... more sausages!
        Oh, I'm in a mess!
No wonder of it : shopping seems immaterial.
Some men can cope with chores. I confess
        I, I myself, I'm much more ethereal.

ON PRINCE WILLIAM LOSING
HIS FIRST BABY-TOOTH

Born out of blood, like a stain
Left where the hawk fells his prey,
The stripped red-raw sinew
Shows in the open mouth.

White, like a tiny vertebra
Severed from its spine,
The hard-gritted biter
Works free, and wobbles

Loose, riven from the jaw.
Spat, smoking, to the pillow,
Trailing its string of blood,
It rips out a baby-cry.

The small white stone saved,
Not for the offal-bin
But under-pillow returned
To await the Tooth Fairy.

and the latest <u>KILLING</u> gave me exactly the same thrill. But, though I have enjoyed this little flurry of murders more than anything in my life, I'm afraid Mary Jane Kelly will have to be my last victim. The trouble is that my identity is now so obvious that, however stupid the police may be, it can only be a matter of time before they arrive to arrest me. I do not regret

HENLEY CENTRAL LIBRARY
OVERDUE BOOKS DEPARTMENT

DEAR : **MR JOHNSON**

The book(s) listed below is/are overdue. We would be grateful if you could return the book(s) to the Library as soon as possible before penalties are incurred. If you wish to extend your borrowing of the book(s), please contact the Library either by telephone or email.

TITLE : **HOW TO BE ME**

AUTHOR : **BERTIE WOOSTER**

IT'S YOUR LIBRARY SERVICE

BOOKS — FREE FOR EVERYONE

DON'T wORRY
YOU'RE NOT
PaRANOid
WE REAlly
ArE
OUT TO Get
yOU

Oh what can ail thee knight at arms
  Alone and palely loitering;
The sedge is wither'd from the lake
  And no birds sing.

Ah what can ail thee wretched wight,
  So haggard and so woe-begone?
The squirrel's granary is full,
  And the harvest's done.

I see a lilly on thy brow,
  With anguish moist, and fever dew;
It looks to me that Benskin's Pills
  Are the things for you.

Sorry Mr Keats I'm afraid I and the rest of the
Marketing Department here at Benskins had visualised
a more aggressive campaign. Hope you can do something
with this.
    J Thompson

just seems to me
a rather elaborate way of
committing suicide, but you're
the President, so if that's
what you want I can
certainly arrange it. There's
a guy called Lee Harvey
Oswald, who I reckon
could be just the sort of
you'll

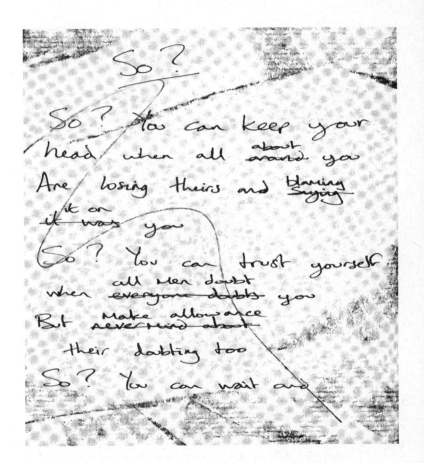

and we at the agency think, to get the message across really forcibly, the campaign poster should be dominated by a head shot of you in uniform with that magnificent moustache pointing outwards above the caption (see sketch below)

JOHN LE CARRÉ

HODDER & STOUGHTON LTD
BOOK PUBLISHERS

14th May 1986.

Dear David,

Many thanks for the manuscript of
the new book, which I read over the weekend
with great pleasure. I'm sure we're on to
another huge international bestseller.

Just a few tiny editorial points.
There are one or two moments in the book
when I could understand exactly what was
going on, so I think perhaps these should
be obscured a bit. Don't you agree?

The page references of these bits are
97 - 101, 211 - 214, and 378 -388.

Sure it won't take you long to sort
them out. We'll talk soon.

All the best,

Yours,

Nigel.

SENIOR EDITOR

ANGLO - SAXON CHRONICLE

10 December 1040

Dear Earl Leofric,

Thank you very much for sending me the tapestry of your wife, Lady Godiva, on horseback, and for your suggestion that it might look good on Page III of the "Chronicle". I regret, however, that this would be against the paper's editorial policy.

Yours sincerely

Eadfrith Angelehieow

Editor

P.S. I apologise that I am unable to return your tapestry herewith, but I'm afraid it seems to have got lost in the Newsroom

WATERSHIP DOWN CENTRAL LIBRARY

OVERDUE BOOKS DEPARTMENT

DEAR : **MR LLOYD WEBBER**

The book(s) listed below is/are overdue. We would be grateful if you could return the book(s) to the Library as soon as possible before penalties are incurred. If you wish to extend your borrowing of the book(s), please contact the Library either by telephone or email.

TITLE : **HOW TO BE ME**

AUTHOR : **GIACOMO PUCCINI**

IT'S YOUR LIBRARY SERVICE

BOOKS — FREE FOR EVERYONE

TRICKETT'SILLUSTRATED DICTIONARY

3 July 2006

Dear Mr Mandelson,

We at Trickett's pride ourselves on the accessibility of our dictionaries, which as I'm sure you know are sold all over the English-speaking world. The principle behind our work is simple: the easiest way for a student to understand the meaning of a word is for him or her to see a picture which describes it. I would therefore be most grateful if you would grant us permission to use a photograph of yourself in our new edition of the dictionary. We have just got to the wor~ OLEAGINOUS and no one in the office can think ~f ~ suitable and informative illustration th~ lizards, but I don't believe ~ slimy and not~ politica~ Europ~ Com~

OUTLINE FOR A NOVEL?

A man has lost
his cow
Precious Ramotswe
finds it for him...

Maybe a bit too
plot heavy...?

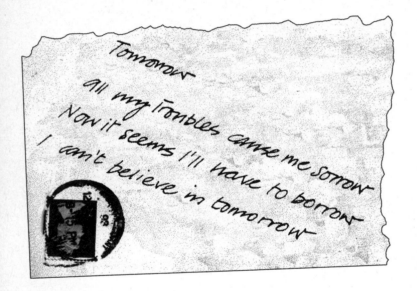

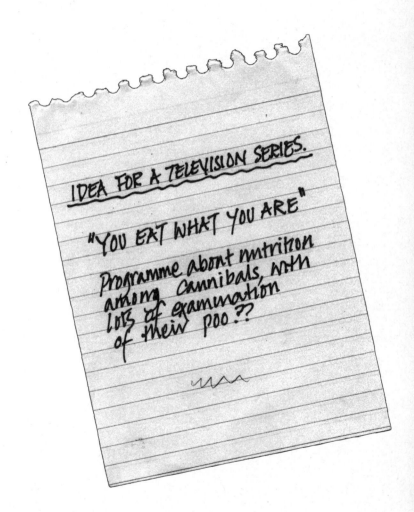

DOCKLANDS CENTRAL LIBRARY

OVERDUE BOOKS DEPARTMENT

DEAR : **SIR IAN MCKELLEN**

The book(s) listed below is/are overdue. We
would be grateful if you could return the
book(s) to the Library as soon as possible
before penalties are incurred. If you wish to
extend your borrowing of the book(s), please
contact the Library either by telephone or
email.

TITLE : **HOW TO BE ME**

AUTHOR : **SIR JOHN GIELGUD**

IT'S YOUR LIBRARY SERVICE

BOOKS — FREE FOR EVERYONE

Dear Signor Buonarroti

You have been recommended to me by the Pope as a reliable painter, and I would like to offer you the job of painting my ceiling.

Please could you let me know what you would charge for the job.

Yours faithfully
Christine Chapel

14th August 1967

Dear Jonathan,
I was, needless to say, very disappointed to hear that you have irrevocably decided to give up the theatre for medicine. I know it must be your decision!

26 Nov. 1974.

Dr Miller

I am so sorry that you have decided to give up your medical work in favour of the theatre. All of us at the hospital

7th May. 1977

Jonathan,
So medicine has finally won out, has it? Well, I can't say I'm surprised, though, of course, you will be much missed in the theatre and your many friends, I'm sure, will

19th March, 1979

Dr Miller,
All of us in the Research Unit were saddened to hear that you have decided finally to give up medicine in favour of the theatre. Needless to say, any research project needs time before it achieves results and we are sorry that following which I feel we

and can fully understand the reason you want to give up the theatre and concentrate on medicine. After all, it's 1982, we're all getting any younger and if you can do more for the benefit

26th November, 1985

Dear Dr. Miller,

So, you have decided that medicine is not for you, after all, and are going back to work in the theatre. None of us can pretend that we share your sense of priorities, but we all hope sincerely that you will not regret decision and

PARADISE LOST
BOOK ONE

Of mans first disobedience, and the fruit
Of that forbidden tree, whose mortal shoot
Brought death into the world, and all our fate
With loss of Eden, till one Man more great
Restore us, and regain the bliss we seek,
Sing, heavenly Muse, that on the secret peak
Of Oreb, or of Sinai, didst exhort
That shepherd, who the chosen seed first taught
In the beginning how the heavens and ground
Rose out of chaos: or if Sion's mound
Delight thee more, and Siloa's brook that ran
Fast by the oracle of God; I can
Invoke thy aid to my adventurous lay
That with no middle flight intends to stay
Above the Aonian mount, but aims to climb
Heights unattempted yet in English rhyme

McTAVISH & McPHEE
TRADITIONAL SCOTTISH OUTFITTERS
PRINCE'S STREET
EDINBURGH

17 May 1932

Dear Mr Mondrian,

Thank you very much for sending us your designs, which we return herewith. Regrettably, we are not currently looking to extend our range of tartans, but I do hope you are successful in placing your work elsewhere.

Yours faithfully,

P.p. H.A.G. McTAVISH
MANAGING DIRECTOR

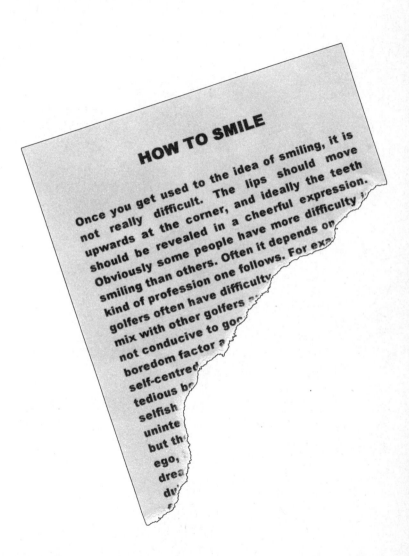

HOW TO SMILE

Once you get used to the idea of smiling, it is not really difficult. The lips should move upwards at the corner, and ideally the teeth should be revealed in a cheerful expression. Obviously some people have more difficulty smiling than others. Often it depends on kind of profession one follows. For ex...golfers often have difficulty...mix with other golfers...not conducive to go...boredom factor a...self-centre...tedious b...selfish...uninte...but th...ego,...drea...du...

XI. THOU SHALT NOT BE SMUG
IF THOU RECKONEST THOU
HAST KEPT ALL THE OTHER
TEN

XII. THOU SHALT NOT GO TO
CHURCH UNLESS IT MEANETH
SOMETHING UNTO THEE

XIII. THOU SHALT NOT EVER SAY
"WOMEN ALWAYS MEAN YES
WHEN THEY SAY NO"

XIV. THOU SHALT NOT SELL
INSURANCE

XV. THOU SHALT GIVE THE
BENEFIT OF THE DOUBT
UNTO ALL (EXCEPT OF
COURSE UNTO THEY THAT
DO SELL INSURANCE)

THE BEAM

At the Close there's a
   breathless hush tonight—
Eight to make & the game
         to win—
A failing pitch and a fading
            light,
The more hour and the last
         man's in.
But since all you'll get is
      a ribbon'd coat,
Or the worthless hope of a
         season's fame,
Tell the Captain you're off
      to have a smoke—
"Give up! give up! and
   stuff the game!"

BRANDO ADVERTISING AGENCY
CORPORATE IDENTITY AND BRANDING

19 August 1981

Dear Brad,

Following last week's brainstorming session on the Nike global image, I agree with you entirely that what the company needs is a universal logo of extraordinary simplicity. I put my creatives on to the task, and after some very late nights and lots of black coffee, they have come up with an idea which in my view ticks all the boxes. It's an internationally recognized symbol which will define Nike quality for generations to come. The artwork is still being refined, but I think the image is so strong that I couldn't resist sending you an advance sketch on the attached sheet.

We at Brando are convinced it's a winner. Let me know your reactions. I'm sure we'll find we're all singing from the same hymnsheet.

Yours ever

CREATIVE DIRECTOR

Beaucoup de gens vont lire ce Quatrain
Quand trois cents ans sont certainement passés
Ils auront tous un Livre à la main,
Qui s'appelle: À Deuxieme Pensées

[An approximate translation of this prophecy would run as follows:

Many people will read these four lines
When at least three hundred years have gone by.
They will all be holding a book
Called: On Second Thoughts...]

ANTHEM FOR OUR BRAVE BOYS

Happy are the boys that meet their fate,

Facing the cannon in this glorious fight.

Happy the soldiers who can breathe their last,

Knowing that the war will not be lost.

For the wise men of Whitehall know what's for the best—

That British boys must fight the German beast.

And what if many die like heroes in a joust,

There's still no doubting that their cause is just.

Some will survive to show their scars with pride,

Some bare their stumps of legs and still be proud,

While others wheeze their words with gas-marred lungs.

That's not the fate for which a soldier longs.

Better by far to die and not to grieve,

But lie embosomed in a foreign grave,

Unmarked perhaps, it does not matter where—

A fitting tribute to the God of War.

Happy those boys who meet their end with zest,

Happy to shout out for their country's glory

That great cry: Dulce et decorum est

Pro patria mori!

Converting to Catholicism

Catholicism is still one of the top religions in the world. Many people would like to convert to Catholicism, but they aren't sure how. Watching someone convert is very powerful and moving. Read all about how to convert to Catholicism by talking to people who have actually done it and hearing at first hand the enormous benefits spiritual and soci...
wh...

and then my mother took me in her arms
and gave me a big hug and said, 'Don't
worry, Dave, whatever happens, Mom'll
always be here for you and
love and support yo
nothing will change
rely on me for
own little boy
foreve
love
kiss

THURSDAY

DEAR PENNY
THAT BLOODY
TROJAN WAR IS
FINALLY FINISHED
SO I SHOULD BE
BACK SOON AFTER
THE WEEKEND.
CAN'T WAIT TO
SEE YOU ETC.
ALL MY LOVE
ULYSSES
XXX

SALVADOR RODRIGUES
Optician & Lensmaker ○○

Avenida Cervantes 235, Barcelona.

23 de octobre de 1904.

Dear Señor Picasso,

　　　We have recently been checking our records, and discovered that, when you ordered spectacles from us four years ago, you were unfortunately given the wrong prescription, and received a pair of blue-tinted glasses prepared for another customer.
　　　We apologise deeply for this mistake, which can be rectified immediately, and hope that it has not caused you any inconvenience.

With profuse apologies,

Yours sincerely,

MANAGER

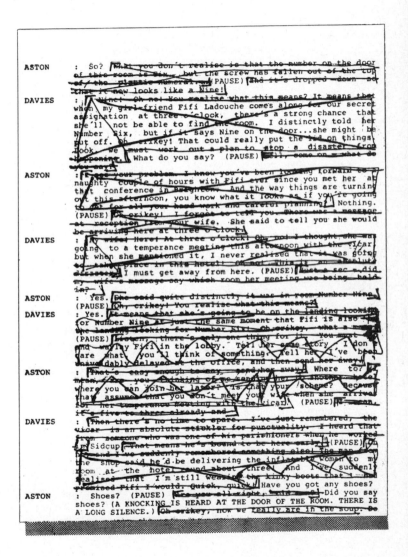

ASTON : So? ~~What you don't realise is that the number on the door of this room is Six, but the screw has fallen out of the top of the~~ (PAUSE) ~~And it's dropped down so that it now looks like a Nine!~~

DAVIES : ~~Nine! Oh no!~~ You realise what this means? It means that when my girlfriend Fifi Ladouche comes along ~~for~~ our secret assignation at three o'clock, there's a strong chance that she'll not be able to find ~~the room.~~ I distinctly told her Number ~~Six,~~ but if ~~it~~ says Nine on ~~the door~~...she might be put off. ~~Oh crikey!~~ That could really put the ~~lid on things.~~ ~~Look, we~~ must work out a plan to ~~stop a disaster from happening.~~ What do you say? (PAUSE) ~~Well, come on - what do you say?~~

ASTON : ~~I see your problem. I know you've been looking forward to a~~ naughty couple of hours with Fifi ever since you met her at ~~that conference in Brighton.~~ And the way things are turning out this afternoon, you know what it looks as if you're going ~~to do for all your hard work and careful planning?~~ Nothing. (PAUSE) ~~Oh crikey! I forgot to tell you. There was a message~~ at reception ~~from your wife.~~ She said to tell you she would ~~be arriving here at three o'clock.~~

DAVIES : ~~My wife! Here! At three o'clock! Oh, no! I thought she was~~ going to a temperance meeting this afternoon ~~with the vicar~~ but when she ~~mentioned~~ it, I never realised that ~~it was going to take place in this hotel! Oh no! This is an absolute disaster!~~ I must get away from here. (PAUSE) ~~Just a sec - did my wife's message say which room her meeting was being held in?~~

ASTON : Yes. ~~She said quite distinctly it was in room Number Nine.~~ (PAUSE) ~~Oh crikey! You realise what this means?~~

DAVIES : Yes. ~~It means that she's going to be on the landing looking for Number Nine at just the same moment that Fifi is also on the landing looking for Number Six. Oh crikey, what a mess!~~ (PAUSE) ~~Listen, there's only one thing for it. You must find and waylay Fifi in the lobby. Tell her some story. I don't~~ care ~~what. You'll think of something. Tell her I've been unavoidably delayed at the office, and then send her away.~~

ASTON : ~~That's easy enough to say. Send her away! Where to? I mean, are you thinking of me landing her in some hotel, maybe, where you can join her later? Is that your scheme? Because that assumes that you won't meet your wife when she arrives for her temperance meeting with the vicar.~~ (PAUSE) ~~I mean, it's five to three already.~~

DAVIES : ~~Then there's no time to spare. I've just remembered - the vicar is an absolute stickler for punctuality. I heard that from someone who was one of his parishioners when he worked in Sidcup. That means he's bound to be here early!~~ (PAUSE) ~~Oh - and I've suddenly remembered something else! The man at the shop said he'd be delivering the inflatable woman to my room at the hotel round about three. And I've suddenly realised that I'm still wearing the kinky boots that I promised Fifi I would. Quick, quick!~~ Have you got any shoes?

ASTON : Shoes? (PAUSE) ~~Are you all right, mate? I - Did you say~~ shoes? (A KNOCKING IS HEARD AT THE DOOR OF THE ROOM. THERE IS A LONG SILENCE.) ~~Oh crikey, now we really are in the soup. So~~

JACKSON POLLOCK

RUMBOLD'S SAFETY PAINTS
1147 EAST GRINDLEY STREET, BROOKLYN, NEW YORK

23rd November 1947

Dear Mr Pollock,

In response to yours of 19th November, I am sorry to hear that you found our paints unsatisfactory. We pride ourselves on the excellence of our products and of course take all complaints extremely seriously. However, I do not believe that our company is at fault in this instance.

You say in your letter that Rumbold's Safety Paints have ruined your latest work, and question the "Non-Drip" quality which features in all our advertisements. I stand by our manufacturing standards, and can only assume that you have been misusing our products, overdiluting them with paint thinner or turpentine. This, I would respectfully suggest, is why your latest composition, "Two Furry Kittens In A Basket", has ended up looking like an explosion in a paint factory.

I am therefore unable to accede to your request for compensation.

Yours faithfully,

MANAGING DIRECTOR

1
6

To The Milkman

God, when creating Man, at once decreed
That ample diet should supply our need
And proper eating, fed by proper food,
Should sickness from our mortal lives exclude.
He also, in His perfect plan, decrees
That thou shouldst carry forth thy milk & cheese
For thee to come unto my door with cream
Is but a part of His Eternal Scheme.
So, three pints, prithee, of thy lacteous flood,
Which willing udders yield to brace our blood,
And of that cheese, whose fame is widely known
Whose secret only Cheddar's sons do own
(Made from the richness of emulsive fats
And churned e'en richer in their ligneous vats)
A half-pound, prithee; and of yellow cream
A half-pint, pray–but not that watery stream
Men know as single–no, the "double" sort
That can be whipped to pinnacles for sport,
As when the mighty waves, by Boreas lash'd,
Rise up in fury, till the rocks be splash'd,
And fearful mariners, that con the sky,
Do shake their head and wink their weather-eye,
All fearful to outface the furious storm,
While quick waves break, & then, as quick, reform
And trembling sailors can be heard to utter–
Oh I forgot–add half a pound of butter.

PARTHENON · PAPYRUS · COMPANY ·

DEAR · MR · PYTHAGORAS ·

MANY · THANKS · FOR ·
SUBMITTING · YOUR · DESIGN · WE · REGRET
TO · SAY · THAT · AS · AN · ENVELOPE, WE'RE ·
AFRAID · IT'S · A · NON-STARTER —
YOURS · SINCERELY
S. MAMOPOULOS

M. Le Docteur Canard
Opposite Notre Dame
Medieval Paris

Dear M. Modo,

The symptoms you describe fit perfectly with the common disease of the ears which is called Tinnitus. There are plenty of proprietary remedies available across the counter at your Apothecary's, but they are all rubbish. May I recommend my own patent medicine, which is distilled from the blo bats with a subtle admix bladders of grass snake

[Egyptologists differ about the precise meaning of this fragment, but the consensus seems to be that it is a shopping list and could be translated approximately as follows:

'1 chicken, 1 game of skittles for the kids, 1 hamburger, 2 more hamburgers (or possibly balls for the game of skittles), 2 fish, 2 meat cleavers, some eye drops (?), cheese and wine, 1 brassiere, 1 Cornish pasty (?), and don't forget the dog food!']

J. B. DEPALDO & SONS

Picture Cleaners & Restorers

17th August 2006.

Dear Mr. Richard,

As requested, we have inspected the picture in your attic, but, since we cannot find any explanation for its rapid deterioration and the apparent aging of its subject, we regret that we are unable to take on the job of its restoration.

With apologies,

Yours sincerely,

GENERAL MANAGER

991 SEX

Screw , bang, bit, ride, grind, knock, mount, score, action, bunk-up, nookie, hump, bonk, jig-a-jig, how's your father, slap and tickle, legover, Ugandan discussions, knee-trembler, tupping, having it off, having it away, getting your end away, getting your rocks off, a bit on the side, a bit on a fork, a stab in the dark with a pork sword.

Wank rub-up, jerk-off, play-off, massage, body rub, hand-job, J. Arthur, frig, flip-off, whack-off, wrist-job, pulling one's pudding, flogging one's mutton, tickling one's mutton dagger, pulling one's wire, pulling oneself off, pumping oneself off, playing with one's knob, shaking one's plum-tree, pulling the goose's neck, slinging one's jelly, flogging one's donkey, bashing one's bishop, trying to knock off the soldier's hat, it's all over my friend.

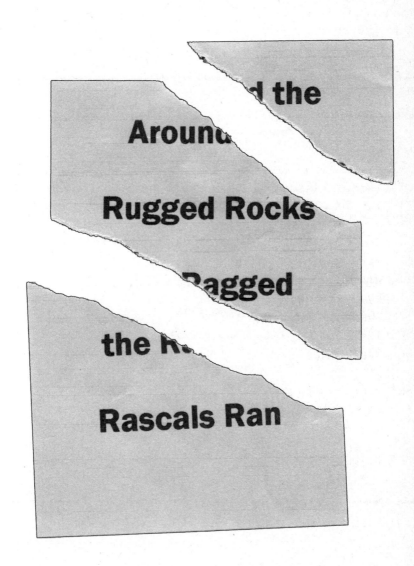

Around d the

Rugged Rocks

Ragged

the R

Rascals Ran

Vienna
11th March 1791.

My Dear Salieri
I've never written a fan
letter before, but then I've never wanted
to. However your music inspires me so
much that I just have to write.
If only I could write stuff as brilliant
as yours

Many Congratulations
your devoted admirer

Wolfgang Amadeus Mozart

GALLIC PROVINCIAL COOKING

FROMAGE DE TETE

INGREDIENTS

I HEAD
I LB CARROTS
I LB ONIONS
I LB LEEKS
III CLOVES GARLIC

METHOD

FIRST CLEAN THE HEAD
AND REMOVE ALL EXTRANEOUS
MATTER (HAIR. ETC) THEN
SOAK IN BRINE FOR THREE
DAYS IN A COOL PLACE, BEFO
BOIL UP WITH THE VEGETAE
CHOPPED UP INTO SMALL PI
PINCH OF SALT AND CRUS
GARLIC UNTIL THE FLESH
SOFT TO THE TOUCH
REMOVE THE OUT
OFF THE BONE
UNTI

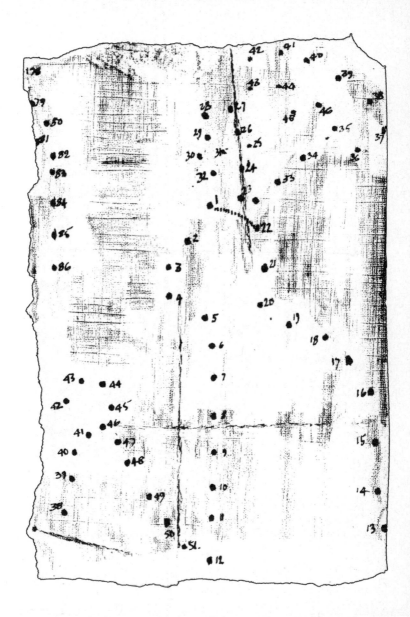

either you do something reall
nice for me {like write the odd
sonnet or something} or else
I'll tell Ann Hathaway what
you did to me last Tuesday
in ye Gents Publick Privie
Stratford-On-Avon I mean whn
I think about it.

Your Dark Laddie

XVIII

Shall I Compare Thee to a

Habitné
dapple bay
Hudson Bay
holiday
Saturday
Christmas day
popinjay
Lump of Clay
Swiss chalet
cheese soufflé
Roundelay
Passion play
Consommé
Breakaway
stowaway
Runaway
Castaway
Negligée
Old Bombay
Hyphooray

POSSIBLES.

DEAR OLD QUEEN ✓

CONQUERING KINGS ✓

DOWN TRAIN ✓

CUNNING STUNTS ✗

A LOVING SHEPHERD ✓

RATE OF WAGES ✓

FRIAR TUCK. ✗

HALF-FORMED WISH ✓

FLATT

CRO

HE

Praxton's Liver pills

3rd November 1869

Dear Mr Stanley

This is to confirm that our company will be happy to sponsor your forthcoming trip to Africa. We are well aware of the publicity value of your finding Dr Livingstone, and are happy to have our names associated with the enterprise.

We do not ask that you should carry any advertising material on your clothes and luggage. Our only request is that at the moment that you finally meet the object of your search you should greet him with the following words:

"Dr Livingstone, I presume you owe your survival in these terrible conditions to Praxtons Liver Pills?"

So long as these words are spoken (in full), we will be happy to pay all your expenses.

Yours Sincerely
J. Garrington
Marketing Manager.

IN FOCUS PRODUCTIONS LTD
10A OLD COMPTON STREET
LONDON W1A 3DS   020 7 534 9827

M Philippe Starck,
45 Rue de Rivoli
346764 Paris
France.

Dear Philippe,

I have received your recent additional sketch for 'War of
the Worlds'. I am afraid all of us here at In Focus feel
that although they are very attractive as objects, as
alien space craft, they are not threatening enough. I hope
you can come up with some alternatives quickly and fax
them to us.

Sincerely yours,

Acme
Firework
Company

ST CATHERINE WHEEL LANE, LONDON E2.

2 April 1826

Dear Mr Stephenson

Thank you very much for showing us the plans for your proposed Rocket. We regret that we cannot possibly see how it is meant to fly, and are therefore unable to offer our backing to the project.

Yours Sincerely

Winton

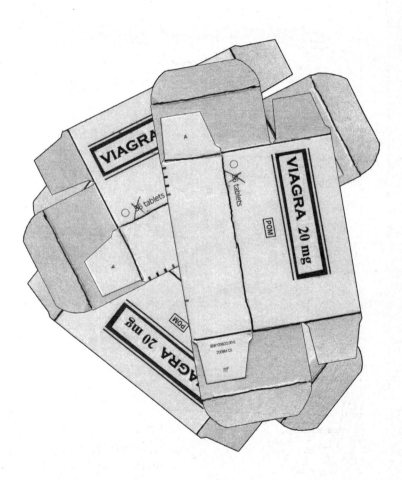

READISMILE CHARM SCHOOL

Sir Alan Sugar
Amstrad plc
169 Kings Road
Brentwood
Essex CM14 4EF

14 May 2006

Dear Sir Alan,

Please find enclosed a cheque for £250, this being a refund of your deposit for the course in which you recently enrolled.

It is very unusual for our instructors to be able to make no headway at all with a client, but in this instance there was general agreement that ending our association with you was the only viable solution.

Yours sincerely,

GEOFFREY TROOP
Managing Director

[This letter has been reassembled from Alan Sugar's office shredder.]

TIME LORD LEGAL SERVICES
PROPERTY TRANSFER AGREEMENT

This agreement being made this seventeenth day of May in the year 2005 between Christopher Eccleston and David Tennant ensures that the said Christopher Eccleston gives and confers to the said David Tennant the property known as the Time And Relative Dimension In Space (commonly and hereinafter referred to as "TARDIS") means of interplanetary and intergenerational vehicular transportation, without qualification or proviso and for all eternity (or until the said David Tennant gets bored and wants to try his luck in Hollywood).

This legal and binding agreement does not, it should be vehemently stressed, confer any ownership or seigneurial rights over the property known as Billie Piper.

DETAILS OF PROPERTY GIVEN AND CONFERRED:

1 Police Box (1950s vintage)
Contents (See Inventory Pages 2 - 4,765,493)

On either side the river lie
Long fields of barley and of rye
That clothe the wold and meet
the sky;
And thro the field the road
runs by
To many-tower'd Camelot;
And up and down the people go,
Ta-tum-ta-tum-ta-tum-ti-toe
But I'm getting bored, and so
I'm sorry—thats Shalott!

Don't be facetious, Alfred
Bloody well concentrate!

UNDER MURDER WOOD
A Whodunit for Voices

FIRST VOICE [very softly]
To begin with the murder. It is dawn, streaky dayburst
bubbling and boring through the bog of the night, lifting
the cloud-cloak, curtain-back and good morning dawning
rise of the slip-shod, slipper-footed, dressing-gown-
garbed, early-morning-tea, slap-of-the-papers-on-the-
"welcome"-mat, light-up-a-cigarette dawn, in the little
town of LLudicrys. All over the town, alarm clocks are
crowing, toothpaste-tubes squeezing, kippers grilling,
cereals soggying, and old men spitting at Jones and
Evans, Vitreous Enamel, Merthyr Tydfil. Every opening
eye and waking heart stirs and stretches and creaks and
uncrumples to the beauty of another do-it-or-drop-it
day. Every eye but one.

SECOND VOICE
Dai the Death alone ignores the morning.

FIRST VOICE
Because he is dead.

SECOND VOICE
Dead down the mine. Down in the doom gloom brown bowel,
deep beneath the stomach of the turgid-stirring, slow-
churning earth.

FIRST VOICE
But what is he thinking, Dai the Death?

SECOND VOICE
He is thinking of nothing, because he is dead. The dead
are tight as misers' purse-strings with the bunched-up
bounty of their bibled thoughts.

FIRST VOICE
But if he were alive, what would he be thinking, Dai the
Death? Only you can hear his thoughts.

FIRST VOICE
…murdered!

TAFF THE TRUNCHEON
"Murdered" is it you say? But that's a terrible word to
be heard by a man still in his flannelette nightgown.
Ring me again, when I have my uniform on.

FIRST VOICE
And as he bustles into black, buckling his belly taut
with the black leather, heaving on hearse-black boots,
hefting his helmet high on the cramped dome of his
cranium…

SECOND VOICE
He hears, wafting through the window, the words of a
morning poem…

MEREDITH
There may be greater towns than ours,
With fiercer and more famous sons,
And higher rates of homicide,
More people armed with knives and guns.

And yet, for me, this blessed place
As scene of crime can have no peer.
Let others inner cities haunt –
I'll still brain all my victims here.

SECOND VOICE
And…

TAFF THE TRUNCHEON
Oh…

FIRST VOICE
Cries Taff the Truncheon

TAFF THE TRUNCHEON
I think that could be a clue.

SECOND VOICE
He would think what he thought day-long down the mine,
as time ticked by, unmarked by the daylight and night,
but by the flickering of his Davy lamp quick across the
slack, as his pick knocked quick at rock blocks of
coal and showers of little bits trickled to his feet.
If he were alive. But he is dead. So what unthinkable,
unthankful thoughts is he thinking now in the coal-hole
gloom of his dusty dreams?

FIRST VOICE
Never such dreams as any that come in the mournful
morning of murder. Never such ends as any that end
in the coal-axe poleaxed through the walnut shell of
his cranium into the unripe soft fruit of his wicked-
dreaming brain. Never such sudden stopping of his
thoughts, his naughty, palm-sweating, hand-groping,
hem-lifting, beard-tickling, dirty postcard pictures
of…

DAI THE DEATH
Blodwyn Jenkins. Oh, Blodwyn, Blodwyn. Blodwyn J…

FIRST VOICE
At the other side of the town, in the tight, cotton-
ticked, up-to-the-chin-tucked, false-teeth-clicked-in-
the-glass, unalarm-clocked silence, Detective Inspector
Taff the Truncheon is woken from a dream of…

TAFF THE TRUNCHEON
Petty thieving, minor traffic infringements, fines for
overdue library books, telling the time to tourists,
commendations for bravery and… and engraved barometer…

FIRST VOICE
…by the thrilling, sleep-killing trill of a truculent
telephone – and the news that…

SECOND VOICE
Dai the death has been…

FIRST VOICE
And he goes out through the trim letterbox-rattling,
catch-clicking, knocker-knocking frame of his front
door...

SECOND VOICE
...to visit Meredith the Murder...

FIRST VOICE
...and says:

TAFF THE TRUNCHEON
I keep thinking there must be a clue in your name,
Meredith, though I'm damned if I know what it is.

FIRST VOICE
But he still arrests him.

SECOND VOICE
Again. As he has done every bloody-bodied day of the
corpse-covered, shroud-shocking year.

FIRST VOICE
And the afternoon died and the thin light fades. And
Taff the Truncheon, roundly righteous, crammed with
complacency, rumbling with rectitude, fulfilled in
flannelette, snores down the slope of his sleep, knowing
that tomorrow he could have a...

TAFF THE TRUNCHEON
...'nother cadaver...

FIRST VOICE
And the sky once again velvets to darkness over the
silver-tapped blood-bath of the little night-winking
town.

IDEA FOR NOVEL...?

GOOD CREATURE,
SMEAGOL (GOLLUM?),
TRIES TO RETURN
MAGIC RING TO ITS
NATURAL HOME. HIS
PROGRESS IS IMPEDED
AT EVERY TURN BY
NASTY EVIL LITTLE
CREATURES WITH
FURRY FEET
(~~BOBBITS?~~ ~~GOBBITS~~
~~FOBBITS~~ HOBBITS✓)
......?

LEO TOLSTOY

[Translation: 'Idea for a short story – WAR AND PEACE']

bob@abgpublishers.com   13 October 2002

To: "Lynne Truss" trussedup@locali.com

Subject: Punctuation Book

Dear Lynne,

I'm interested in your idea for a book about punctuation, though I'm not sure about the title you suggest, EATS SHOOTS AND SAPLINGS. Any other ideas?

All the best,
Bob

...r kind invitation for me to

...i'm afraid I have to say no, because I

...to have to be very selective with the kind of work I take on. I don't want to get a reputation as the kind of celebrity who just does anything that'll keep her face on the nation's television screens. After all, I do have a very high IQ and it's a matter of integrity me not to be seen as a pushover in matters o...

cheap in any way or...

devalue t...

art...

Venator : I thank you, good master. for this observation. But I would know of you what shall be done when your Angling is of no avail and you catch naught?

Piscator : Marry Sir, now must you learn, what many old anglers know right well, that at some times, and in some waters, be the rod never so supple, be he that bears it never so subtle, and be the bait never so succulent, no fish is to be got. And when that be your fortune, must you take this course:

You must Lie.

Venator : Did you say "lie" good master?

Piscator : Sir I did say so: and by so doing, you will follow the authority of Aristotle, of Pliny, of Gesner, and of many others of credit. And before I go farther in my discourse, let me tell you, good scholar, of the divers kinds or sorts of lies with which you must arm yourself.

And, first, for the bigness of your catch. Concerning which, I shall give you this direction: that your fish shall thrive in bigness by much discourse. It is said by Jovius, who hath writ of fishes, that in an inn in Italy, he did hear of a Carp of more than an hundred pounds weight.

Venator : But, good master, did he see this prodigy with his own eyes?

Piscator : Nay, good scholar, because you, that are but a young angler, know not what Lying is. I will now teach it to you. Let your lies be never of the fish that is to be seen, but always of The One That Got Away; and let this fish be fully the length of your arms extended sideways; for it has been observed by Aldrovandus and divers other

OSCAR WILDE

LADY B: What lost both your parents
Mr Worthing? Bad luck
What lost both your parents
Mr Worthing? That's unfortunate
It'd be bad enough if you'd only
lost one parent, Mr. Worthing.
Losing two's really tough
To lose one parent, Mr. Worthing is
rotten luck. To lose two's even
worse
To lose one parent, Mr Worthing may
be considered rotten luck. To lose
both's even worse.
To lose one parent, Mr Worthing may
be regarded as rotten luck. To lose
both looks even worse
To lose one parent, Mr Worthing, may
be regarded as unfortunate. To lose
both looks like divine retribution.
To lose one parent, Mr Worthing, may
be regarded as a misfortune; to
lose both looks like the kind of
thing that only happens to someone
who's really accident-prone.

161

NG RECORD OF
YOUR TRIP:

BROAD WITH
TAPESTRY

BY
GET WEAVING OF
BAYEUX

VIRGINIA WOOLF

[Unfortunately there is nothing available, since every last shopping list has already been published.]

I wandered lonely as a cloud
That rains upon the
Daddies and the Mums.
When all at once I saw
                a crowd.
A host, of gold
                chrysanthemums.

I'm sorry William,
I really don't think you
should go with this one.
It's not one of your best.
            Dorothy

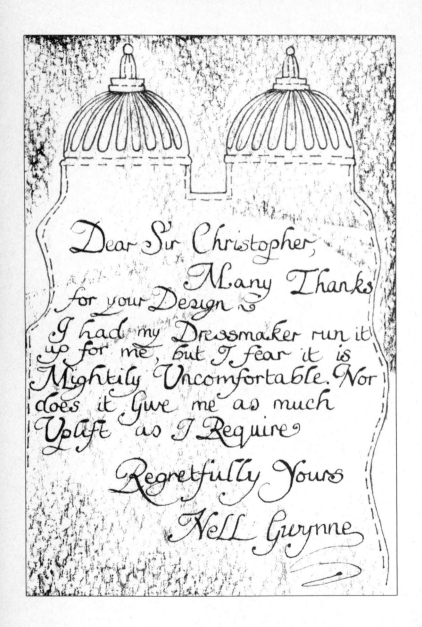

Dear Sir Christopher,
            Many Thanks
for your Design

I had my Dressmaker run it
up for me, but I fear it is
Mightily Uncomfortable. Nor
does it give me as much
Uplift as I Require

        Regretfully Yours

                Nell Gwynne

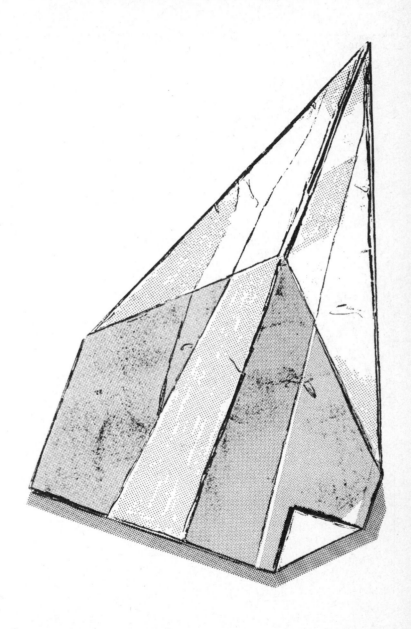

Other titles from Summersdale

The
Wind-up
Letters

Mark Hebblewhite

The Wind-up Letters

Mark Hebblewhite

£6.99 Paperback

ISBN: 1 84024 534 9
ISBN 13: 978 1 84024 534 9

From a man with far too much time on his hands comes this collection of barmy correspondence, guaranteed to put a smile on the face of even the most dedicated customer services assistant.

Whether he's appealing to the British Lubrication Federation for advice on resolving his cat flap predicament or making an enthusiastic request to Tiffany & Co for Tiffany's autograph, Mark Hebblewhite knows how to make a nuisance of himself. If you've ever wanted to ask McVitie's whether a custard cream is really just an albino bourbon, this book has the answer – as well as the answers to some other questions you might never have thought to enquire about.

Mark Hebblewhite has been a lifeguard, a waiter and an international personal banker, as well as a vegetarian butcher and a folder of cardboard boxes in a soap powder factory. He lives on the Isle of Man.

Tish and Pish

How to be of a speakingness like Stephen Fry

A delicious collection of sumptuous gorgiosities

by Stewart Ferris

Tish and Pish
How to be of a speakingness like Stephen Fry

Stewart Ferris

£7.99 Hardback

ISBN: 1 84024 466 6
ISBN 13: 978 1 84024 466 3

The English tongue has never tasted more delicious than in the mouth of Stephen Fry: his chokingly brilliant sesquipedalian prose is like a shaft of sunlight through the drizzle of quotidian language.

Now, with this bound monograph, we can all emit a similarly exquisite effulgence and enjoy the bright shaft of Stephen Fry locution in the privacy of our own smallest pavilion. May his shaft continue to pleasure us for many years to come. After all, what could be fluffier?

Stewart Ferris is the author of more than twenty books, including *How to be a Writer* and *The Little Book of Flirting*. He has penned several feature film screenplays and his television scriptwriting includes a series of the children's animation *Pokémon*.

'This is an incredibly entertaining read and great fun for any Stephen Fry fans or budding social climbers!'

Student Direct

Brit Wit

The perfect riposte for every social occasion

Edited by
Susie Jones

Brit Wit
The perfect riposte for every social occasion

Edited by Susie Jones

£7.99

ISBN: 1 84024 415 1
ISBN 13: 978 1 84024 415 1

Ever been at a loss for words? Ever wished that the perfect wry remark (or putdown) would spring to mind?

The great, the good, the intellectual and the downright insulting can all be found in *Brit Wit*.

Densely populated with wonderful one-liners from such formidable figures as Churchill and Shakespeare to more recent luminaries of British stage, screen and society including Michael Caine, Victoria Wood, Eddie Izzard and John Lennon, *Brit Wit* celebrates all that makes Britain brilliant.

'Plumped with zippy one-liners and comebacks for any occasion, this book collects the best zingers from the greatest minds in British history'

The Good Book Guide

'If you prefer your humour condensed into one-liners try *Brit Wit*, a beautifully presented catalogue of jests, asides, ripostes and insults'

The Daily Mail

www.summersdale.com